Read before p...

SOME PAGES ARE MEANT TO BE READ BY HIM ONLY OR HER ONLY. PLEASE, FOLLOW THE INSTRUCTIONS. DON'T PEEK OR ELSE YOU WILL SPOIL ALL THE FUN FOR YOURSELVES!

WE SINCERELY HOPE THAT OUR XMAS SEX GAMES & CHALLENGES WILL SPICE UP YOUR SEX LIFE AND LET YOU EXPLORE YOUR SEXUAL DESIRES AND FANTASIES. TO MAKE SURE THIS HAPPENS, TALK TOGETHER AND SET YOUR BOUNDARIES FIRST. PLEASE REMEMBER: ALL THE CHALLENGES, GAMES AND ACTIVITIES ARE ONLY SUGGESTIONS AND LEAVE PLENTY OF ROOM FOR YOU TO CHOOSE WHATEVER FEELS MOST COMFORTABLE. BE NAUGHTY, BUT PLAY SAFE ;). HAVE A VERY MERRY CHRISTMAS!

24

Days to go

YOU BOTH READ THE NEXT PAGE

Hitting the jackpot

Play 'rock, paper, scissors'. The winner
rolls a dice*. Go to the last pages to
see what lucky sex position you've got.
*If you don't have a dice, you can
use any online dice roller.

23

Days to go

SHE READS THE NEXT PAGE

Madame Claus

Slip some of your lingerie in his pocket, briefcase or bag before he leaves for work. Wait 2 hours and unless he finds out first, ask him in a text if he's noticed anything unusual. Then, send him a dirty text or a naughty recording saying what you will do to him when he gets back.

22

Days to go

HE READS THE NEXT PAGE

Naughty or nice?

PUT ON A SANTA HAT OR A WHOLE
SANTA COSTUME (IF POSSIBLE). INVITE
HER TO SIT ON YOUR LAP AND ASK HER
IF SHE'S BEEN NAUGHTY OR NICE THIS
YEAR. DELIVER A RELEVANT
REWARD OR PUNISHMENT.

21
Days to go

YOU BOTH READ THE NEXT PAGE

Creative Santa

Invent a Christmas-themed sex position. Come up with a suitable name for it. Think of the best possible place for doing it. Now, try it out.

20
Days to go

SHE READS THE NEXT PAGE

A mistletoe trap

Hang mistletoe in a place where it can be barely spotted. Lure him under the plant and refuse to release him unless he satisfies you.

19
Days to go

SHE READS THE NEXT PAGE

Feast for the eyes

PUT YOUR SEXY CHRISTMAS LINGERIE ON. TAKE
A CHAIR AND PUT IT NEXT TO A MIRROR. MAKE
HIM SIT IN IT. STAND IN FRONT OF THE MIRROR
AND START TAKING OFF YOUR CLOTHES SLOWLY
SO THAT HE CAN ENJOY WATCHING YOUR GORGEOUS
BODY FROM DIFFERENT ANGLES. THIS WILL TURN HIM
CRAZY BEFORE YOU GO ON TO THE MAIN COURSE.

18

Days to go

HE READS THE NEXT PAGE

Whet her appetite

Tease her all day without having sex. Here are a few suggestions: whisper dirty things in her ear randomly, tell her how horny she makes you, ask about her recent sexual fantasy, try sexting (no explicit photos unless asked for). Then, take her for a night ride to see Christmas lights. Pull over at some point and see what happens.

17

Days to go

HE READS THE NEXT PAGE

The South Pole

TONIGHT YOU'RE GOING TO THE SOUTH POLE ;).
LET HER CHOOSE WHAT SHE CRAVES MOST.
YOU CAN SPOIL HER WITH MORE THAN ONE.

☐ USE A SEX TOY OF MY CHOICE

☐ MASSAGE MY G-SPOT

☐ BLINDFOLD ME

☐ CUFF OR TIE ME

☐ MAKE IT SUPER SLOW AND SENSUAL

☐ SUCK LIGHTLY ON MY CLIT

☐ PLAY WITH MY ANUS

☐ OTHER _____

16

Days to go

SHE READS THE NEXT PAGE

Candy cane

THIS CANDY CANE AIN'T GONNA LICK ITSELF.
LET HIM CHOOSE WHAT HE CRAVES MOST.
YOU CAN SPOIL HIM WITH MORE THAN ONE.

- ☐ BE ENTHUSIASTIC AND EAGER
- ☐ KEEP EYE CONTACT
- ☐ SWALLOW EVERY DROP
- ☐ TALK DIRTY TO ME

- ☐ LET ME GIVE YOU A FACIAL
- ☐ PUT AN ICE CUBE IN YOUR MOUTH
- ☐ LET ME FINISH ON YOUR BOOBS
- ☐ OTHER _____

15

Days to go

He reads the next page

A sensual tickler

Get her naked with your mouth only.
Take Christmas tinsel and stimulate her
body until she asks for something more.
You can try going for some of the hottest
female erogenous zones, such as : the nape
of neck, belly, inner thighs or feet.

14

Days to go

SHE READS THE NEXT PAGE

Christmas prep

Make him leave to get something for you.
Get naked and put your heels on. When he
gets back, pretend to be busy doing some
christmas preparations. You can tease him
a bit more. Grabbing something off
the floor should do the trick ;).

13

Days to go

YOU BOTH READ THE NEXT PAGE

Can you give me a hand, honey?

PLEASE EACH OTHER WITH YOUR HANDS ONLY AND
TRY TO FINISH AT THE SAME TIME. ALTHOUGH IT'S
A HARD CHALLENGE, ACHIEVING IT CAN BE REALLY
REWARDING. PRO TIP: USING LUBE CAN COME IN HANDY.

12

Days to go

HE READS THE NEXT PAGE

The more, the merrier

Experiment with sex toys. First, find out what she's comfortable with. If you've never explored this area together, you can start with a vibrator and stimulate her nipples or clit. If she's not shy, let her play with a toy of her choice while you watch or satisfy her. If she feels more adventurous, you can try double penetration, a wall mounted dildo or some submission or domination games.

11

Days to go

SHE READS THE NEXT PAGE

A spanktula

It's time for some naughty cooking. Put on an apron and nothing underneath. What will be absolutely necessary is a silicone or a wooden spatula. To make it more fun, you can use plastic wrap as handcuffs, put oven mitts under your knees or take a pastry brush to let him apply lube. This should be enough to get your creative juices flowing. Remember: you make all the rules!

10

Days to go

SHE READS THE NEXT PAGE

Santa's secret

You will need a bed and warm chocolate, whipped cream, maple syrup or any other favorite edible substance you can write with. Ask him to lie on his belly. Sit on his legs and write a secret sex message on his back. Make sure he's got it. Then, lick the message off. That's a perfect opportunity for you to share something you've always wanted to try, but never dared to say.

9

Days to go

HE READS THE NEXT PAGE

Wrap it up

Wrap yourself like a Christmas gift. You can make it funny or hot. To make her smile, you can go with a Christmas-themed ribbon and a big bow attached to your penis. To make yourself look smoking hot, use some thick satin ribbon for the wrap-up. Pro tip: lying under a Christmas tree works wonders.

8

Days to go

YOU BOTH READ THE NEXT PAGE

No pillow talk

DECORATE YOUR ROOM WITH CHRISTMAS LIGHTS.
FIND AS MANY PILLOWS AS YOU CAN AND DIVIDE
THEM EVENLY. YOU'RE GONNA HAVE A PILLOW FIGHT.
THE WINNER GETS TO PICK HOW TO USE THE PILLOWS.
IF YOU ARE OUT OF IDEAS, GO TO THE LAST
PAGE TO GET SOME INSPIRATION.

7
Days to go

SHE READS THE NEXT PAGE

Naughty fluff

Get a pair of red or white fluffy handcuffs.
Put your sexy nightgown on. Cuff his hands
to bed. Tell him how naughty you feel today.
Lift up your nightgown and sit on his face.

6
Days to go

YOU BOTH READ THE NEXT PAGE

Winter lottery

You both need 3 pieces of paper and a pen.
Secretely write down 3 things you'd like to try.
Fold each paper wish and put all of them in a jar
Draw them one by one and choose the hottest
sex wish you're both keen on trying.

5

Days to go

HE READS THE NEXT PAGE

I can't wait

Bring her to the edge of an orgasm and back off. Repeat this two times more and finally let her climax. If you can't read her body cues before she comes, talk to her first and agree on some sign so that you can stop at the right moment.

4

Days to go

HE READS THE NEXT PAGE

Hot bubble bath

Run her a bath, light scented candles,
put out the biggest and fluffiest towels,
pour her some mulled wine and play
romantic Christmas music. You can
add some christmassy decorations
to create more Christmas vibe.

3
Days to go

SHE READS THE NEXT PAGE

I'm snowed under

CHRISTMAS EVE IS AROUND THE CORNER.
YOU MUST BE AWFULLY BUSY AND QUITE
STRESSED. ENJOY THIS OPPORTUNITY TO
HAVE QUICK AND PASSIONATE SEX.
PUT YOUR DRESS ON AND DRAG HIM
SOMEWHERE QUIET. START MAKING OUT,
BUT DO NOT LET HIM UNDRESS YOU. PICK
THE RIGHT MOMENT TO WHISPER TO HIS
EAR: "PULL MY PANTIES TO THE SIDE".

2

Days to go

SHE READS THE NEXT PAGE

A dirty letter

DESCRIBE YOUR CHRISTMAS SEX WISH IN EVERY DETAIL.
LET'S SEE HOW GENEROUS SANTA IS GONNA BE THIS YEAR.

_____

_____

_____

_____

_____

_____

1
Day to go

HE READS THE NEXT PAGE

A dirty letter

DESCRIBE YOUR CHRISTMAS SEX WISH IN EVERY DETAIL.
LET'S SEE HOW GENEROUS SANTA IS GONNA BE THIS YEAR.

_____

_____

_____

_____

_____

_____

Merry Christmas!

Your lucky position

1. REVERSE COWGIRL

YOU SIT ON TOP OF HIM, FACING HIS LEGS. YOUR LEGS ARE BENT IN KNEES AND FEET STRETCHED OUT ALONG HIS BODY. YOU HAVE MORE CONTROL OVER THE PACE, RHYTHM AND DEPTH OF PENETRATION. YOU CAN EXPERIMENT WITH LEANING FURTHER BACK OR FORWARD TO EXPERIENCE ALL ANGLES THIS POSITION HAS TO OFFER. HE CAN PUT HIS HANDS ON YOUR WAIST TO HELP YOU MOVE UP AND DOWN.

2. THE VALEDICTORIAN

IT LOOKS LIKE MISSIONARY POSITION, BUT IT'S WAY NAUGHTIER. RAISE HER LEGS, SPLIT THEM AND PUT HER ANKLES ON YOUR SHOULDERS SO THAT HER LEGS FORM A "V". IF SHE ISN'T FLEXIBLE ENOUGH, SHE CAN BEND HER LEGS IN KNEES. TO MAXIMIZE HER PLEASURE, INSTEAD OF JUST THRUSTING, TRY LEANING FORWARD AS CLOSE TO HER AS YOU CAN GET TO GRIND YOURSELF AGAINST HER CLIT WHILE YOU STAY INSIDE HER.

Your lucky position

3. The pretzel

She lies on her right side. You kneel down and straddle her right leg, then lift her left leg and curl it around your left side. This position makes it easy to fondle her breasts or stimulate her clit while you penetrate her.

4. Doggy style

She bends over, gets on all fours, facing away from you. You get down on your knees and enter her from behind. It's a classic, yet there is plenty of room to spice it up. Grab her hair, spank her, tie her hands or hold them and pull her into you. She can be more dominant and push back on you while you rub on her clit for more pleasure. You can do it standing, on stairs, some piece of furniture, a yoga ball, etc. The sky's the limit.

Your lucky position

5. The spoon of pleasure

She lies back, extends one leg straight, bends the other at the knee and lifts it up. You lie on your side close to her. Then, you slip your hand under her head and bend it at the elbow in order to have access to her breast. You can push from behind, caress her thigh and work your way down to her clit.

6. Passionate wrap-around

You sit on the edge of bed with your legs bent and feet on the floor. She sits on your laps, facing you, then slides into you. Your palms cover her buttocks and move them up and down. This position gives you a lot of intimacy as it lets her wrap her shoulders around you, keep eye contact and kiss you passionately. To make it naughtier, she can place her palms on your knees and lean back to let you kiss her breasts.

No pillow talk

Slide a pillow under her butt during missionary to deepen penetration or hit her g-spot. Putting a pillow under her chest during doggy style will give you easier access or give her more stability to push back from. By lifting her hips, you get different angles during other positions. Placing a pillow under your neck makes eye contact easier and leaves no neck strain. Pillows can keep your knees pain-free, they work well when you're different heights. You can also put them on the floor to have discreet sex. A lot of people fantasize about sex in a pillow fort. Maybe it's a turn-on for your partner.

Printed in Great Britain
by Amazon

31232729R00031